Remembering
Honolulu

Clifford Kapono

TURNER
PUBLISHING COMPANY

Sitting to the rear of 'Iolani Palace in this 1880s view, the crater Puowaina is a sacred site that was used by the pre-contact Hawaiians as a place of human sacrifice and ali'i burials (chiefs' burials). Rainwater runoff from the crater to the basin of Honolulu helped create the large, freshwater harbor around which the city would develop. Since 1949, Puowaina, or Punchbowl, has been home to the National Memorial Cemetery of the Pacific.

Remembering

Honolulu

Turner Publishing Company
www.turnerpublishing.com

Remembering Honolulu

Copyright © 2010 Turner Publishing Company

All rights reserved.
This book or any part thereof may not be reproduced or transmitted
in any form or by any means, electronic or mechanical, including
photocopying, recording, or by any information storage and retrieval
system, without permission in writing from the publisher.

Library of Congress Control Number: 2010932276

ISBN: 978-1-59652-703-4

Printed in the United States of America

ISBN: 978-1-68336-838-0 (pbk.)

CONTENTS

Here on the grounds of 'Iolani Palace in the 1880s, King Kalakaua and Queen Kapi'olani stand in the foreground in front of the Coronation Pavilion, with Colonel Charles H. Judd and Antoinette Swan, wife of Lyman Swan, just behind them.

Acknowledgments

With the exception of touching up imperfections that have accrued with the passage of time and cropping where necessary, no changes have been made. The focus and clarity of many images are limited to the technology and the ability of the photographer at the time they were recorded.

This volume, Remembering Honolulu, is the result of the cooperation and efforts of many individuals, organizations, and corporations. It is with great thanks that we acknowledge the valuable contribution of the following for their generous support:

Friends of ʻIolani Palace
Hawaii State Archives
Hawaii State Library, Regional Branch at Hilo
Library of Congress
University of Hawaii at Manoa:
Hamilton and Sinclair Libraries
Department of Economics
College of Tropical Agriculture and Human Resources

We would also like to thank the following individuals for valuable contributions and assistance in making this work possible:

Kathleen Camara
Ritchie Henderson
Markham and Luana Rosehill

This book is dedicated to my five children: Lisa, Cliff, Christian, Lauren, and Aloha, who are the source of my inspiration.
—*Clifford Kapono*

PREFACE

From the time of its earliest inhabitants, centuries ago, the Honolulu coastline offered two contrasting assets of natural beauty—the oceanfront at Waikiki, comfortable for the shallow-draft outrigger canoes used by the native population, and the deep harbor created by the waters of the Nuʻuana Valley, favored later by foreign vessels. The first of these to arrive was the English sailing ship Butterworth, captained by William Brown, in 1794. Hawaiians living and fish-farming along the water's edge referred to the bay and its vicinity as Ke Awa O Kou (the harbor of Kou) but Brown called it Fair Haven, a name that stuck when later translated into Hawaiian as Honolulu.

While Kamehameha I solidified a hard-won reign over a unified Kingdom of Hawaii, until his death in 1819, the harbor served a briefly lucrative sandalwood trade and the first stirrings of a whaling industry. Arriving in 1820, New England missionaries immersed themselves in the life of the islands and carved their mark on Honolulu's landscape with small wooden mission houses to which would be added, through their own and their children's industry, large commercial buildings. Between the 1820s and the 1850s, the population of Honolulu grew from about 3,000 to about 11,000 residents. During this time, a number of men with names that would dominate public life in Honolulu for the next century arrived in the islands.

Honolulu's attributes spurred the political interest of European nations and of Hawaii's near neighbor to the east, the United States, which established diplomatic and trade relationships with Hawaii by entering into a commerce treaty in 1826. In 1843, through the machinations of a local British official, Hawaii briefly came under British rule, but the home government quickly renounced the claim and reaffirmed Hawaii's sovereignty. In a speech to commemorate the occasion, Kamehameha III spoke the phrase that would become Hawaii's motto: *"Ua mau ke ea o ka ʻaina i ka pono"* ("The life of the land is perpetuated in righteousness").

In 1850 Honolulu officially became a city and the capital of the Kingdom of Hawaii when Kamehameha III relocated the capital from Lahaina on Maui. This geographical shift significantly impacted the Protestant missionary community, whose members had positioned themselves alongside a ruling class of native Hawaiians, the aliʻi, as council and spiritual advisors during Hawaii's transition from a feudal society into an internationally recognized member of the family of nations, governed as a constitutional monarchy. The missionaries' direct influence was on the wane, however, and as the years passed those without financial support either returned to New England or settled into the general population of the islands, some to prosper in private business.

Honolulu's importance continued to grow with the whaling industry, requiring expansion of the harbor facilities and government infrastructure. But the shipping trade also brought to the islands diseases against which Hawaiians had no defenses. Consequently King Kamehameha IV and his wife, Queen Emma, lobbied door-to-door to raise funds for a new hospital to intervene in the accelerating depopulation of the native Hawaiians. The hospital was finished in 1859 and dedicated as the Queen's Hospital at Honolulu.

The rapid expansion of the petroleum industry after 1859 eroded demand for whale oil, and the Civil War further depleted the number of whalers doing business at Honolulu. Pro-Union Americans with political influence in the kingdom looked for ways to support the Northern states, and one way was to fill the demand for sugar, a Southern product. Hawaiian sugar became incredibly profitable during the Civil War, earning a competitive place on the world market, establishing an ever more firm hold on Hawaii's domestic economy, and setting the stage for conflict that lay just ahead, much of it to be played out in easy reach of Waikiki and the Nuʻuanu-replenished harbor.

—*Clifford Kapono*

Honolulu's most recognized landmark, Diamond Head, an inactive volcano crater seen here in 1859 from along the Waikiki shoreline, was given its erroneous name by British sailors fooled by calcite crystals that sparkled from it in the midday sun. The traditional name for this crater is Leʻahi (the brow of the yellowfin tuna). Formed an estimated 300,000 years ago, the crater was used as a military lookout beginning in the early 1900s. Named a national natural landmark in 1968, Diamond Head is now a state monument and is used by various state and federal governmental agencies.

The Life of the Land

(1850–1899)

In the 1800s, when this photo was taken, Hawaiians relied on Waikiki as an important fishing site, its waters teeming with a variety of fish and lobster available as fresh seafood daily. Canoes like this one would often go several miles out to sea. The large paddle blades served for steering and paddling through high surf.

Built in 1816 along Honolulu's shoreline, the small fort depicted in this painting eventually became a jail for rowdy sailors. It was destroyed in 1857 as part of the harbor's improvement plan but would be remembered in the name of Honolulu's Fort Street, a principal artery running from downtown to the base of the bay where the old fort once stood. In 1968, most of the street became a pedestrian mall.

Built in 1845, the original 'Iolani Palace was this wooden structure first utilized as the royal palace by Kamehameha III. It was eventually destroyed by termites. With construction of the second and final 'Iolani Palace, completed in 1882 under Kalakaua, a smaller wooden structure would be built as residence for the monarchs, providing them with a more informal setting for their daily living than was commanded by the palace with its rigid formalities.

In 1865, when this view of Queen Street was captured, Honolulu faced many of the problems of a fast-growing city. Overcrowding and random building densities provided opportunity for squalor and disease to spread through certain parts of the town.

Nineteenth-century Honolulu had its own version of the Barbary Coast, with drunken sailors, prostitutes, and cardsharps, and wild cattle running through the streets. The missionaries had influence, but there was a breaking point to every moral regulation they imported. In 1865, when the Tom Moore Tavern was photographed, Honolulu was a dangerous city.

Dedicated in 1874, Aliʻiolani Hale was originally intended as a palace for Kamehameha V, who commissioned two Australian architects to design it, but the building was repurposed as government office space before it opened. By then, Kalakaua was king, and Kamehameha V was honored by a tower frieze reading "Kamehameha Elima, Ka Moi." During the overthrow of the monarchy in 1893, the provisional government read its declaration in Aliʻiolani Hale. Today the building houses the state supreme court, the state law library, and a judiciary history center, with the much-photographed statue of Kamehameha I in front.

Seen here in all its original splendor, 'Iolani Palace, the official royal residence, was built between 1871 and 1882. The kingdom's last two monarchs, King Kalakaua and his successor, Queen Lili'uokalani, reigned here.

In the distance behind ʻIolani Palace rise the mists of Nuʻuanu, its pattern of ridges and valleys creating streams that flow down from this natural amphitheater and continue along the dry coastal flats, eventually reaching the natural harbor of Honolulu. From Nuʻuanu, also, the northwest trade winds blow, creating rainclouds along the Koʻolau mountain range that feed the running streams.

The coronation of King Kalakaua and Queen Kapiʻolani on February 12, 1883, nine years into Kalakaua's reign, was a significant departure from the ceremonies traditionally attending accession to the royal throne of the Kingdom of Hawaii. The structure seen here, the Coronation Pavilion, was built for this event that melded European formalities such as a coronation ball and state dinner with Hawaiian traditions such as hula dancing and a luʻau. The celebration culminated February 14 with the unveiling of the statue of Kamehameha the Great that stands in front of Aliʻiolani Hale.

Presented to King Kalakaua on the occasion of his fiftieth birthday, these wooden, finely-honed bowls were symbols of power and respect given to acknowledge the king's position in society as aliʻi.

Waikiki held a special place in the minds and hearts of native Hawaiians. As a traditional place of worship and everyday living, Waikiki, seen here in 1880, provided a means for Hawaiians to maintain contact with the 'aina (land) with which they felt cosmologically knitted as one. It was not uncommon for the royal families to spend time tending to their farms in Waikiki, as traditional practice dictated, not as laborers but as stewards of the cherished land of their forefathers.

The raw natural wealth of Waikiki can be seen clearly in this nineteenth-century setting from before construction and tourism. As pristine as this view is, the entirety of the Hawaiian Islands was once in this same condition. Fortunately, a few remote corners have escaped the overcrowding and remain undeveloped. What Walden Pond was to Henry David Thoreau, Waikiki is to its people.

Founded in 1858 by partners Charles Reed Bishop and William A. Aldrich, the Bishop and Company bank is seen here shortly after the firm's new building opened in 1878. Designed by architect T. J. Baker in the Renaissance Revival style, the building became a reference point for political and commercial power in Hawaii and the continental United States. Charles Reed Bishop, husband of Princess Bernice Pauahi Paki Bishop, wielded great power in Hawaii but ran his bank, the forerunner of First Hawaiian, with a strong sense of fairness and integrity.

Shipping was a major industry for Honolulu, with tremendous profits to be made along the lanes of the Pacific. But S. G. Wilder, the founder of the interisland Wilder Steamship Company, did not confine himself to oceangoing enterprises. He was also active in the development of rail lines in Honolulu and elsewhere in the Hawaiian Islands. The sign in the shop window at left indicates his business was the local agent for cables and galvanized wire rigging from John A. Roebling's Sons and Company, of Brooklyn Bridge fame.

Clearly there was profit in the cable sales trade and the sundry other enterprises in which Wilder and Company engaged, as evident by this dramatic step up in the size and solidity of its business facade.

The three-story building seen across Honolulu Harbor in this 1880 view housed the sailmaking business of J. M. Oat. His son, J. M. Oat, Jr., ran a printing business. Among the younger Oat's publications, he collected and reprinted the Hawaiian Gazette's news accounts of Queen Emma's funeral in 1885.

The merchandise broker John Thomas Waterhouse established his import business in 1851. Marketing goods both wholesale and retail, the J. T. Waterhouse firm, operating out of the building seen here at right in 1884, satisfied local needs for everything "from a needle to an anchor" and also did private mail-forwarding in the years before a reliable government postal service had been developed.

The Kwong Hip Lung Company, at far left, was among the many Honolulu businesses owned or managed by Chinese residents. In the background, at right, stands the second Kaumakapili Church, with its distinctive twin steeples. The church was dedicated in 1888, during Kalakaua's reign, but destroyed in the Chinatown fire of January 1900.

Members of the Kawaiahaʻo Church in Honolulu were accustomed to worshipping inside grass huts when, in 1836, King Kamehameha III arranged for construction of a new place of worship. Begun a year later, the coral stone Kawaiahaʻo Church, seen here, took five years and the collective effort of more than a thousand men to build. At the church in 1843, Kamehameha III spoke the words that are now Hawaii's motto: "Ua mau ke ea o ka ʻaina i ka pono" ("The life of the land is perpetuated in righteousness"). King Kamehameha IV and Queen Emma were married at Kawaiahaʻo Church, where services are still conducted in Hawaiian.

Tall ships and steam-powered sailboats line the Honolulu waterfront and navigate the harbor in this 1885 view. The large schooners were for heavy, transoceanic commerce; the smaller, steam-and-sail vessels ferried passengers interisland and carried lighter goods. Here, the two steamers heading out of the harbor are, left to right, the Mikahala and James Makee of the Inter-Island Steam Navigation Company.

To help celebrate Kalakaua's fiftieth birthday in November 1886, incandescent lamps were turned on at 'Iolani Palace, making Hawaii's royal residence the first to be illuminated by electricity. The government followed with an electrification plan for the city as a whole, to be powered by Nu'uanu Valley water. Honolulu's first electric streetlights were in place by March 1888 (switched on by Princess Ka'iulani), and within a year a number of homes and businesses were also enjoying the novel wonder of electric light.

King David Kalakaua's fiftieth birthday was celebrated over many days through festivities held in and around 'Iolani Palace. Kalakaua had a driving passion to revive Hawaiian cultural practices lost to the influence of Western missionaries, while still maintaining a strong affinity for the Western-style education and scientific inquiry he witnessed in his travels around the world.

The tall ships that lined Honolulu Harbor for nearly a century brought building materials and supplies from the West Coast of the United States in exchange for goods such as raw sugar and pineapples. Tall ships built in Oregon, for example, carried lumber from the Pacific Northwest to Honolulu, where many ships would be found loading and unloading at any given time in the harbor. The shoreside labor required was staggering.

Hawaiians with their abstract perspective were fascinated by the written word. Newspapers were a modern marvel that held more fascination than mechanical inventions. The Pacific Commercial Advertiser, the ancestor of today's Honolulu Advertiser, was founded in 1856 by Henry M. Whitney and was sold to the sugar magnate Claus Spreckels, a royalist, in 1880, or possibly to Kalakaua's adviser Walter M. Gibson. The paper's pro-monarchy editorials were deplored by many resident American businessmen, and the paper was sold to the Hawaiian Gazette in 1888, with the combined papers then passing to Lorrin A. Thurston, a leader of the annexation movement, in 1895.

The combination of services offered by this business on Fort Street points to the future profitability of a funeral home: furniture, undertaker, and embalmer. The rise in population called for an increase in mortuary services, and perhaps was a factor in the idea put forth around that time to locate a cemetery on Puowaina.

At the funeral service for King Kalakaua in 1891, the grounds are filled with mourners outside ʻIolani Palace, which would stand as his legacy, the only royal residence on American soil and symbolic of Hawaii's era of independence. At odds during his reign with the majority of the American and European businessmen in Hawaii, Kalakaua became a champion of the people, calling for the resurrection of various cultural arts and practices.

Kalakaua's cabinet members stand next to kahilis, the black-feathered royal banners signifying the presence of an ali'i (king) in 1891. With the king dead, Hawaii found itself in a precarious position. It had never been governed without a reigning patriarch. Queen Lili'uokalani would succeed Kalakaua, but these were the kingdom's last days.

One of many Scotsmen to visit Honolulu was the author Robert Louis Stevenson, who became a personal friend of King David Kalakaua and Princess Ka'iulani while on an extended stay in Hawaii in 1889. Stevenson is seen here relaxing in Hawaii with his family. Princess Ka'iulani was the daughter of Archibald Scott Cleghorn, a financier from Edinburgh who served as O'ahu's last royal governor. While in Hawaii, Stevenson wrote the short story "The Bottle Imp," inspired by the Hawaiian stories he heard while visiting at Ainahau, Cleghorn's Waikiki home.

'Iolani Barracks, or Halekoa (Warrior House) was designed by the German immigrant Theodore Heuck, who was commissioned by King Kamehameha V, and was constructed in 1870. The small garrisons of native Hawaiian soldiers housed there were the reigning monarch's royal guards. During the overthrow of 1893, the small infantry unit would have likely proved no match for the larger, more equipped force of 162 members of the U.S. Navy and Marines that came ashore from the USS Boston, had armed conflict occurred.

Bicyclists, barefoot children, and promenaders make the most of a shaded Hotel Street here in the late 1890s.

On Hotel Street in 1898, local Hawaiian flower vendors would set up directly on the sidewalk, where potential customers could walk by and admire the garlands of fresh-strung, scented flower lei. For the Hawaiian, a lei was a gift of aloha. Its significance was in the moment, that for a short time the flower's beauty would enhance the natural essence of the person, and together they were linked to the land, the people, and the universe.

'Iolani Barracks is seen here in 1895. That year Robert Wilcox, a part-Hawaiian in Queen Lili'uokalani's court, organized an armed revolt against the government of the Republic of Hawaii, established after the queen was deposed. Wilcox had led a similar revolt in 1889 against the 1887 constitution that had been forced on King Kalakaua. Both failed rebellions are remembered as romantically courageous, however futile.

Prince Jonah Kuhio Kalaniana'ole and his wife, Elizabeth, are shown here seated in a Quadricycle. Prince Kuhio was imprisoned for nearly a year for his role in the 1895 Wilcox rebellion. Elizabeth Kahanu Woods visited the prince in prison, and they married after his release, in 1896. After a period away from Hawaii, Prince Kuhio returned and served for many years as Hawaii's delegate to the United States Congress.

Seen here on Nuʻuanu Street, as viewed from Hotel Street, Love's Bakery was founded by Robert Love, who arrived with his family in 1851 from Australia. A native of Glasgow, Scotland, he started his bakery a month after setting foot in Honolulu. Bakers in nineteenth-century Honolulu primarily served the shipping trade.

In 1888, Hawaiian Tramways Company launched an islandwide transit operation using mule-drawn cars, as seen here on Beretania Street. Making the city more accessible by these railcars allowed people to live farther away from the ocean, in places where traditional housing was built and flourished. As the population moved further inland, water access was a major concern, so the valleys of Nuʻuanu and Manoa were often the first choices.

The Coronation Pavilion at 'Iolani Palace, where King Kalakaua and Queen Kapi'olani were crowned on February 12, 1883, is sometimes referred to as the 'Iolani Bandstand. The structure continues today as the site of the Royal Hawaiian Band, which plays music written by the monarchs of the Kingdom of Hawaii, in particular Queen Lili'uokalani, who wrote "Aloha 'Oe" (or "Aloha Oe") and many other Hawaiian songs.

Sanford B. Dole was the Territory of Hawaii's first governor under the Organic Act, serving from 1900 to 1903. He was born a citizen of the Kingdom of Hawaii to missionary parents in 1844 and was a cousin of James Dole, the famous pineapple magnate. After the 1893 overthrow of the monarchy, he was named president of the Republic of Hawaii. When the United States annexed Hawaii, Dole was named territorial governor and is seen here being sworn in.

TERRITORIAL TRANSITION

(1900–1919)

Built in the Renaissance Revival style, the Bishop and Company Building with its arched windows stands behind recently strung wires in this turn-of-the-century view.

The turn-of-the-century waterfront provided jobs that were close to the ocean and to the excitement of sailing ships and new merchandise, and that attracted many to the harbor in search of work. Adults and young children brought their tin lunchpails, ready to work a full day, dressed in appropriate workclothes—coats and hats but not necessarily shoes, which were not mandatory and which many did not wear.

Located at the corner of Fort and Hotel streets, the three-story Mott-Smith Building, at left, was named for John Mott-Smith, Hawaii's first dentist. After arriving in 1851 from California, he also served as a government official and for a time as editor of the Hawaiian Gazette. In 1897, a few years before this photo was taken, the Mott-Smith became one of the first two buildings in the islands to boast an electric elevator.

When originally constructed in 1870, 'Iolani Barracks housed the small number of soldiers who made up the Kingdom of Hawaii's Household Troops. Disbanded by Kamehameha V for a time after the troops seized the barracks in a mutiny, the force was later reconstituted under Kalakaua as the Household Guard, which it remained until the end of the monarchy. Seen here in the early 1900s, the barracks served various purposes, military and otherwise, during the territorial period.

In this turn-of-the-century view of Honolulu Harbor, foreign influence is dramatically clear in the number of tall ships in the distance and the large homes altering the landscape, likely reflecting the wealth accumulated by the sugar barons and those of their society.

The first Japanese bank to achieve any permanency in Hawaii, the Yokohama Specie Bank (Yokohama Shokin Ginko) was an overseas financial agent chartered by the Imperial Japanese government. Opened in 1910, the Honolulu branch was designed by the prolific architect Harry Livingston Kerr. After the bombing of Pearl Harbor, the Alien Custodian Agency confiscated the bank, leaving some customers to spend years trying to recover their seized assets, on which the government paid no interest until lawsuits long after the fact forced the issue.

Though Hawaiian Tramways Company had operated a mule-drawn trolley line since 1888, the rival Honolulu Rapid Transit Company prevailed in a race between the two to be the first to offer electric railway service to the city. While Hawaiian Tramways rushed to lay double tracks on the streets it already controlled, Honolulu Rapid Transit opted for an electric line from Thomas Square to the King Street Bridge and debuted its service on August 31, 1901. This electric trolley was photographed the following year at Waikiki and Hotel.

Waikiki Beach, seen here around 1904, had always provided Hawaiians with every need they could imagine—food grown in gardens, fish raised in ponds, fruit from trees lining the beach, and endless surf on white sunny sand for idling away their leisure time.

The first hotel resort at Waikiki, the Moana Hotel opened on March 11, 1901, the brainchild of the affluent Waikiki resident Walter Chamberlain Peacock. Despite such modern amenities as telephones in the guest rooms, the Moana struggled initially, and Chamberlain sold it to Alexander Young in 1905, about the time of this photo. Run by Young's estate after his death in 1910, the Moana was sold in 1932 to the Matson Navigation Company.

Hawaiian Electric Company (HECO), whose powerhouse is seen here, grew profitable in part because the electric utility business was so capitalintensive it was difficult to sustain competition. Granted a ten-year exclusive franchise in 1893, HECO agreed to pay the government 2.5 percent of its gross earnings and to provide power wherever requested in Honolulu, though the service remained unaffordable to many. The company expanded the power grid to Waikiki by 1897.

A Honolulu ship chandlery and hardware store, E. O. Hall & Son was established in 1852 and became prosperous providing equipment for the sugar industry, building material for the ʻIolani Palace, power generators for electricity, and eventually even 1,400 gallons of "Eggshell Mill White" paint for the Aloha Tower. E. O. Hall is also remembered for having printed an edition of the Bible translated from English to Hawaiian. A devout Christian, he earned a reputation for being honest and above reproach.

An executive with Honolulu Iron Works and an investor in the sugar industry, Alexander Young parlayed his profits from those endeavors to build the 300-room Alexander Young Hotel in downtown Honolulu, at Bishop and Hotel streets. The building, its interior seen here, cost $2 million and opened in 1903. Two years later Young bought the Moana Hotel at Waikiki.

By 1901, two or three passenger steamers, on average, arrived from San Francisco every week, discharging visitors in need of accommodations. From its opening in 1903, Honolulu's premier hotel was the Alexander Young; at six stories, the hotel was also the city's tallest building until surpassed by the Aloha Tower in 1926.

Seen here around the turn of the century, Fort Street then as now cut through the heart of downtown Honolulu and intersected with Chinatown. In December 1899, the bubonic plague broke out in Chinatown, ultimately claiming hundreds of lives as the terrible disease, often called Black Death, spread through the district's overly congested quarters. Government authorities restricted Chinatown residents to their area or sent them to quarantine camps, then ultimately resorted to a program of controlled fires to contain the epidemic. The first fire was set on New Year's Eve.

On the morning of January 20, 1900, one of the controlled fires set in Chinatown to combat the bubonic plague escaped containment. The fire spread quickly, and soon the entirety of Chinatown was in flames. While their homes and businesses burned, the district's residents were held back from fleeing, due to the plague restrictions. Miraculously, no lives are known to have been lost in the fire, but with Chinatown razed, ill feelings festered as some in the white business community saw an opportunity to expand into the area. This view of Honolulu shows the city after the Chinatown fire, with the shell of the ruined Kaumakapili Church visible at upper-right.

In addition to housing an ice cream parlor, as seen here in 1903, the Elite Building was where the Honolulu chapter of the YWCA rented its first office space after forming in 1900. Completed in 1899, the Elite Building was located on the Bishop Street site of the present Remington College.

This panoramic view from around 1910 shows the sheer scale of industry active on the Honolulu waterfront in the early years of the twentieth century.

Baseball was introduced to Hawaii by Alexander Cartwright, one of the game's founding pioneers, who settled in Honolulu after a brief sojourn in the California gold rush of 1849. By 1910, when this photo of a Honolulu team was taken, baseball had found its place as a popular Hawaiian sport.

In 1910 the government went to great lengths to promote Hawaiian flowers in the mainland United States, and also in Canada, Mexico, Europe, and even South Africa, highlighting the whole affair through a lavish floral parade. This particular flower float represents the recently opened Fort Shafter. The float stands in front of the original site of the Kamehameha Schools, built by Charles Reed Bishop to fulfill the wishes of his late wife, Princess Pauahi Bishop, who bequeathed her large estate for the establishment of an educational institution for Hawaiian children.

O'ahu's sugar plantations had their own rail lines to bring sugarcane from their fields to their mills. The first common carrier to connect the plantations to Honolulu Harbor was Oahu Railway and Land, founded by businessman Benjamin Franklin Dillingham. The line was built primarily for hauling cargo but offered passenger service as well.

Founded in Honolulu in 1854 by David M. Weston, the Honolulu Iron Works Company and Flour Mill only briefly focused on milling flour. Like most large Honolulu enterprises of the day, the machine shop grew with the sugar industry, and in 1900 it expanded into a new facility at Kakaʻako. With ship-repair services added to its portfolio, Honolulu Iron Works employed a sizable workforce, as seen here.

Both E. O. Hall and his son William were involved from the outset in the introduction of electric power to Honolulu. As a firm, E. O. Hall & Son sold generators to private homes and businesses before the establishment of a central plant, and William Hall participated in the initial partnership from which Hawaiian Electric Company emerged in 1891.

In this 1915 view of Hotel and Alakea streets, the humble Honolulu Automobile Stand resides kitty-corner from the majestic YMCA Building.

In this 1916 photo, the streetcar at left is passing in front of Cunha Music Company, an enterprise founded by the songwriter and Hawaiian music ambassador Albert "Sonny" Cunha. Combining ragtime and other mainland musical styles of the day with island music and mostly English lyrics, Cunha helped develop a popular sound that came to be known as hapa haole (part white) music.

Plantation workers load sugarcane onto carts here in 1917. The sugar industry in Hawaii profited from cheap labor that in the pre-territorial years included contract labor. The Honolulu factors and banks that were connected to this enormously profitable industry became internationally recognized, controlling investments and influencing trade in the Pacific. Under these conditions, sugar dominated Hawaii's economy, influencing government with the same heavy hand with which it controlled its labor force.

Heavily loaded plantation cane cars line up for the round-the-clock milling of cane. Once it had been hand-cut in the fields, the cane was lugged to and stacked on these rail cars by those on the hapai ko gang and trundled to the mill. Cut cane had to be processed within an 18-hour window to retain its sugar content.

Suggesting the scale of enterprise that linked the sugar industry with the shipping industry at Honolulu, this 12,000-ton steamer is being loaded with sugar from the smaller steamers lined alongside it. In 1919 the average price of sugar was two and a half cents per pound.

Seen here in 1917, the First National Bank of Hawaii opened in 1900 at the corner of King and Fort streets as one of eight banks in Honolulu. Established by a group headed by Colonel G. W. MacFarlane, the bank was to act as a financial agent for the new territorial government. Its first year, the bank reported capital stock of $500,000 and surplus capital of undivided profits amounting to $289,000.

Lydia Paki Kamakaʻeha Liliʻuokalani, Hawaiiʻs last reigning monarch, was laid to rest after her death November 11, 1917, with a funeral held at ʻIolani Palace. Queen Liliʻuokalani reigned from 1891 until 1893, when the monarchy was overthrown by those seeking to institute the Republic of Hawaii. She stepped aside to avoid bloodshed and under protest, expecting reinstatement by the U.S. government. During an attempt by Robert Wilcox and others to restore the monarchy in 1895, weapons were found buried at Liliʻuokalaniʻs home, though she denied any knowledge, and for a time she was imprisoned. In her lifetime she wrote more than 150 songs, some of them written during her incarceration.

Officials descend the steps at 'Iolani Palace on June 22, 1918, the day Charles J. McCarthy was appointed territorial governor.

Construction workers put finishing touches on the Theo H. Davies Building as it nears its 1921 completion. Davies arrived in Hawaii in 1857 and rose from the level of a shipping clerk to build an empire based on interests in the sugar business and, early on, as an original partner with Alexander Young and others in Honolulu Iron Works.

Sugar, Sand, and Surf

(1920–1940)

The same Alexander Young who was a partner with Theo H. Davies in Honolulu Iron Works bought the Moana Hotel in 1905. Later, the Matson Navigation Company would expand its holdings in the hotel industry to include the Moana, seen here, which Matson would purchase in 1932.

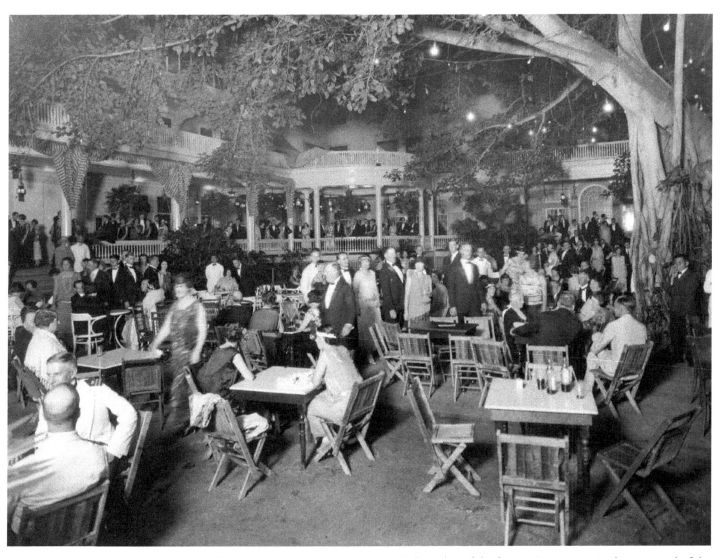

Lightbulbs hang from wires strung beneath the branches of the famous Banyan tree in the courtyard of the Moana Hotel in 1920. Planted in 1904, the tree has since grown to a height of over 75 feet and was selected as a Millennium Landmark Tree by the America the Beautiful Fund in 2000. The Millennium Landmark Tree project was established to protect and preserve one tree in every state.

Wedged between the seawall and a thicket of cars, a large crowd of citizens lines the waterfront for an unidentified occasion in 1921.

Among the oldest Catholic cathedrals in the United States, Our Lady of Peace Cathedral in Honolulu was built on land granted to the Catholic mission by Kamehameha III. Blessed and dedicated in August 1843, the cathedral has long been the focal point of Catholicism in Hawaii, which initially faced strong opposition from Protestant missionaries closely allied with the Hawaiian monarchs. Catholic priests were expelled for a time in the 1830s. In 1839, largely at the insistence of the French government, Catholics were granted the right to worship, and the cathedral land was given.

Prince Kuhio died on January 7, 1922, just months after Congress passed the Hawaiian Homes Commission Act. This photo is from his funeral at Kawaiahaʻo Church. He is interred at the Royal Mausoleum at Nuʻuanu.

These one-man fishing canoes, seen around 1922, have the traditional Hawaiian outrigger design that includes a round hull for quick turning— making for a handy fishing vessel along the rugged coast and a great surfing canoe for open-ocean fishing.

The sun sets on the southwest shore at Waikiki Beach. This six-man Hawaiian outrigger canoe seems to be out for surfing on the change of tide. The outside swells are gaining on the starboard side, while the outrigger is strategically placed on the port.

Stories are told that in 1897, the sugar baron Charles M. Cooke and others took their money out of the Bishop and Company bank, by then owned by Samuel Damon, and paraded it downtown in a wheelbarrow before arriving at Fort and Merchant streets, where Cooke and others established the Bank of Hawaii. Giving islanders a sense of wealth, the Bank of Hawaii encouraged personal deposits from the large working-class community in Honolulu and elsewhere. Here the bank interior is crowded for promotional pageantry of some type.

A German ship captain who settled in Honolulu in 1849, Heinrich Hackfeld operated a general store that grew into a successful trading, real estate, and sugar investment enterprise, later passed on to family members. During World War I, Hackfeld and Company, then managed by George Rodiek, was seized by the American Alien Office Custodian, and its assets wound up in the hands of business rivals who reformed the company under the name American Factors and ran it from this headquarters.

Seen here on a seaplane during his tenure as Hawaii's sixth governor, Wallace R. Farrington, at left, was a newspaperman turned politician who also served as mayor of Honolulu. He arrived from New England in 1894 as editor of the Pacific Commercial Advertiser, later affiliating with the Evening Bulletin. He was appointed governor in 1921, and during his administration Congress passed the Hawaiian Homes Commission Act, which aimed at returning native Hawaiians to their land.

During the 1920s, a marked schism in lifestyle existed between plantation workers and city dwellers—including their entertainment options. In this 1924 view of Fort Street, the two-year-old Princess Theater can be seen in the distance, while Victrolas are advertised at left.

Viewed here while under construction in 1925, the ten-story Aloha Tower in its early years was a welcoming harbor landmark and the tallest structure in Honolulu. One of a number of important projects overseen by Honolulu mayor John H. Wilson, an engineer by trade, the tower opened in 1926. Because of its high visibility, the Aloha Tower was camouflaged during World War II.

Crisscrossed trolley tracks mark the corner of Hotel and Fort streets here in the 1920s.

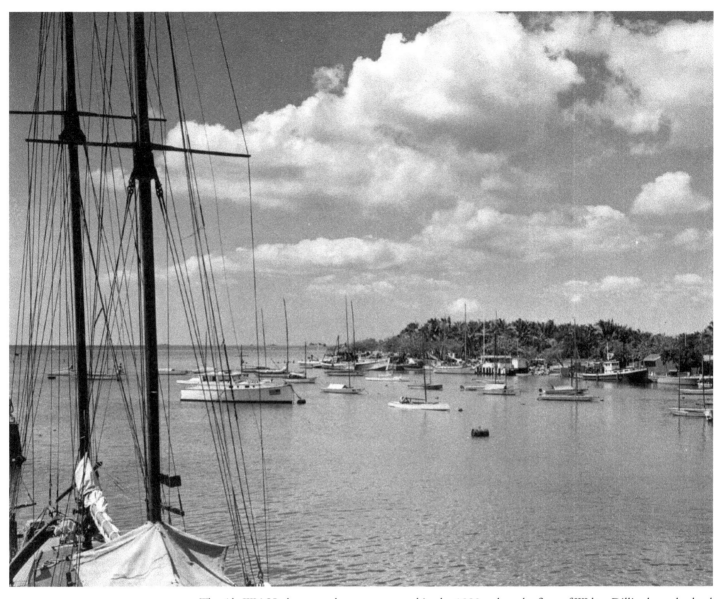

The Ala Wai Harbor, seen here, was created in the 1920s when the firm of Walter Dillingham dredged a canal to flush rainwater from swampy, mosquito-ridden Waikiki. Mayor John H. Wilson promoted a contest to name the new canal, and the winning name was Ala Wai.

The typical Honolulu business luncheon has changed much from the time of this scene photographed at the Haleiwa Hotel. Meetings concerning land and commerce issues now include women and Asians, who are involved at every level of the new service economy.

Still under construction here in 1926, the Royal Hawaiian Hotel, nicknamed the "Pink Palace," opened its doors on Waikiki the following February. The hotel was developed by the Matson Navigation Company to complement its luxury steamer service. It was not the first Royal Hawaiian Hotel, however. The original Royal Hawaiian opened in downtown Honolulu in 1872 and was later bought by Alexander Young.

Traveling to Hawaii by passenger ship, well-heeled visitors such as these found their way to the Royal Hawaiian Hotel not by accident but by design of its parent firm, the Matson Navigation Company. No one of the hotel's early guests was more famous than Franklin D. Roosevelt, the first president of the United States to visit Hawaii. During a four-day visit in July 1934 he enjoyed a bit of deep-sea fishing and planted a kukui tree on the grounds of 'Iolani Palace.

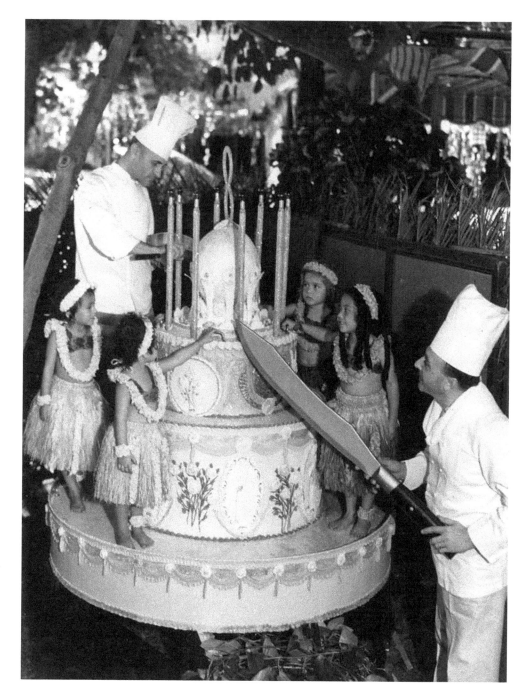

Young hula girls help decorate a cake taller than they are at the Royal Hawaiian Hotel in 1935.

Aside from the shape of surfboards and the materials used to make them, nothing much about them has changed through the years. The boards are still shaped by hand, and young surfers still ride the waves at Waikiki. This board's flat, round nose and wide tail block were perfect for the south-shore surf. Waikiki has many different types of waves to ride, ranging from small tubes on the inside, like the almond-shaped barrels at Baby Queens, to the larger, full-faced waves found at Canoes or Poplars during a big summer swell.

Here on November 9, 1925, the Bank of Bishop's new 75,000-square-foot Damon Building, named for bank executive Samuel Damon, opened at the corner of King and Bishop streets. With the banking business growing in tandem with the sugar and pineapple industries, the Bank of Bishop (formerly Bishop and Company) merged in 1929 with the First National Bank of Hawaii, the First American Savings Bank, the Army National Bank of Schofield Barracks, and the Baldwin Bank of Maui. Renamed Bishop First National Bank of Honolulu, it recorded assets of more than $30 million.

The Bank of Bishop's Damon Building stands in this view with its Greek columns representing strength and permanence.

Seen here at the corner of Merchant and Fort streets, the Judd Building was designed by Oliver Traphagen and opened in 1898. The Bank of Hawaii operated out of the Judd in the early decades of the twentieth century, as did Alexander & Baldwin.

Not long after the Bank of Bishop opened the Damon Building, the rival Bank of Hawaii moved from
the Judd Building into this new headquarters.

The Dillingham Transportation Building is seen here not long after its completion in 1929. The Dillingham name had been prominent in Honolulu since Benjamin Franklin Dillingham arrived in the 1860s. He later founded the Oahu Railway and Land Company.

A San Francisco institution founded in 1861, the high-end retailer Gump's developed a strong association with the Pacific Rim. The Gump's outlet seen here in Honolulu featured "hollow tile" in its design.

Heavily uniformed in tropical heat, the policeman seen here directing traffic at the intersection of Fort and King streets needed his umbrella. The Honolulu Police Department was officially established in 1932, though its origins date to government legislation enacted in 1846 under the reign of King Kamehameha III.

The Portuguese introduced the braguinha to Hawaii in the late 1800s. The small, stringed instrument caught on like wildfire, and according to one legend, Hawaiians likened the quick-fingered technique of playing it to a 'ukulele (leaping flea), and the name stuck. The popularity of the ukulele led to a cottage industry with great export potential, especially when a craze for Hawaiian music swept the mainland in the early twentieth century. Here ukuleles are being crafted at a shop in 1926.

On August 16, 1927, shortly after Charles A. Lindbergh made his historic transatlantic flight, a group of aviators took off from Oakland Airport in a dangerous race to Honolulu sponsored by James D. Dole, the pineapple magnate. The team of Art Goebel and William V. Davis, Jr., took home the $25,000 given by Dole as first prize after a flight of 26 hours, while Martin Jensen, of Honolulu, and Captain Paul Schluter received $10,000 for finishing second. Here, Jensen and Schluter's Aloha has come to rest at Wheeler Field.

A crowd of onlookers awaits the arrival of the Dole flight contestants. During the race, two planes disappeared over the ocean, as did a third plane that departed the next day to search for them while also attempting to reach Honolulu. In all, ten people died in the Dole race or events surrounding it.

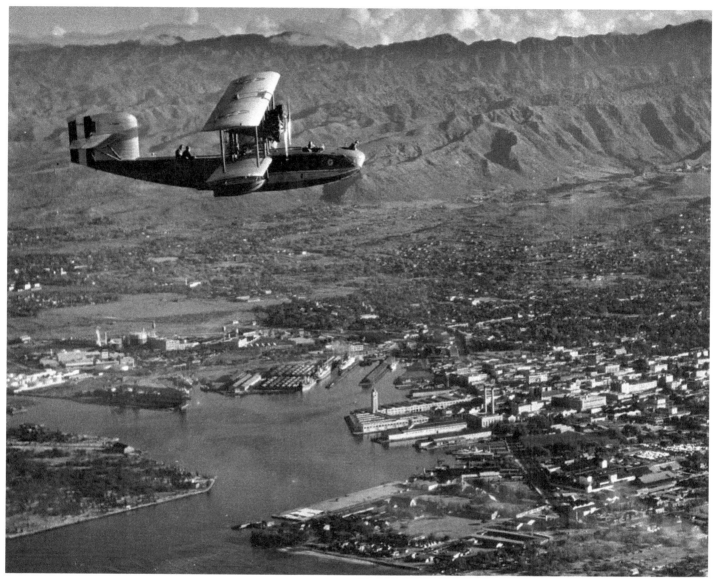

The drama and tragedy of the Dole race, and the adventurousness of the fliers, ultimately helped pioneer safe air travel to Hawaii. The pilot of this seaplane has a clear view of Honolulu Harbor and the Aloha Tower. Looking down, it would have been difficult for him to imagine the growth to come.

In the 1920s, the roads in Honolulu were few and not in the best of condition, since most of them were dirt roads, but an automobile like one of these parked outside the Royal Hawaiian Hotel was a necessity for the wealthy.

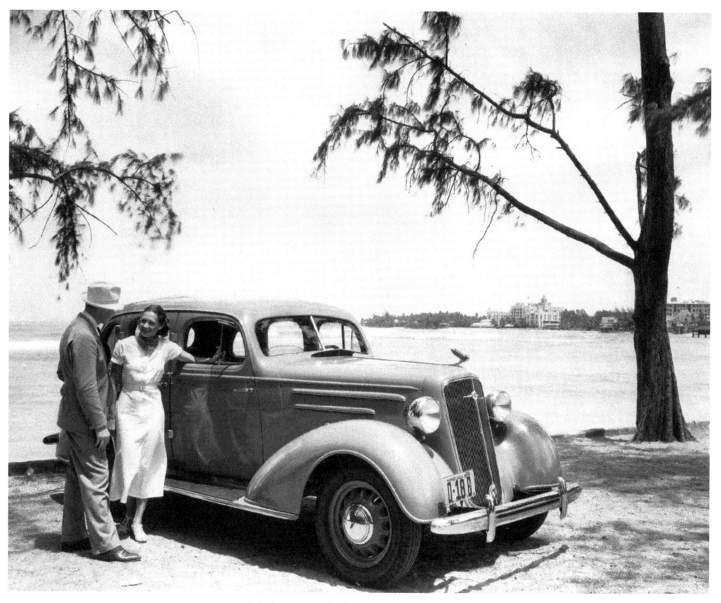

Honolulu has always had a fascination with new things and the latest fashions, cars included. This Chevrolet was a popular model of the times; today, fancy imports and high-end luxury cars are seen all over Honolulu, most stuck in traffic.

Seen here in 1930, these are the famous Waikiki beach boys, acclaimed for their expert waterman skills and their charm, who plied their trade on the beach fronting the Royal Hawaiian and Moana hotels. Teaching visitors to surf, catch waves in outrigger canoes, and enjoy the easygoing Hawaiian culture, they became unofficial ambassadors, adding to the mystique and glamour of Hawaii's travel industry.

The Pearl Harbor Navy Yard is seen here at its entrance in the 1930s, by which time the facility included an air station and a submarine base.

In 1934 a schoolboy looks out over Honolulu from atop Puowaina, where marked stones indicate the distances to various landmarks. By then Honolulu was no longer an isolated spot on an island out in the middle of the Pacific Ocean. In three fast decades since annexation the city had grown into a major U.S. port with a sizable military presence. Some residents saw Honolulu as continuing to provide the prosperity that they and their families had long known; for others, it was still a servant's perspective. Either way, the view had become more interesting than ever.

Cars follow a trolley down King Street in 1934, a year notable, among other milestones, for the election of Duke Kahanamoku, the Olympic gold medalist and surfing popularizer, to the office of sheriff of Honolulu.

As a Honolulu industry, skipjack tuna fishing grew from the level of local-market commerce to eventually supply the Hawaiian Tuna Packers cannery, where this hardworking tuna packer probably was photographed.

Many Japanese laborers started small businesses in Honolulu, as did many Chinese. Some succeeded in much larger enterprises. The grandson of a Chinese immigrant, Chinn Ho was born in Waikiki and eventually became a self-made multimillionaire, developing the Ilikai hotel-condominium high-rise and becoming the first Asian director of the Big Five firm Theo H. Davies and Company.

Located by the harbor, the Dillingham Transportation Building glows at night in 1934, five years after its completion.

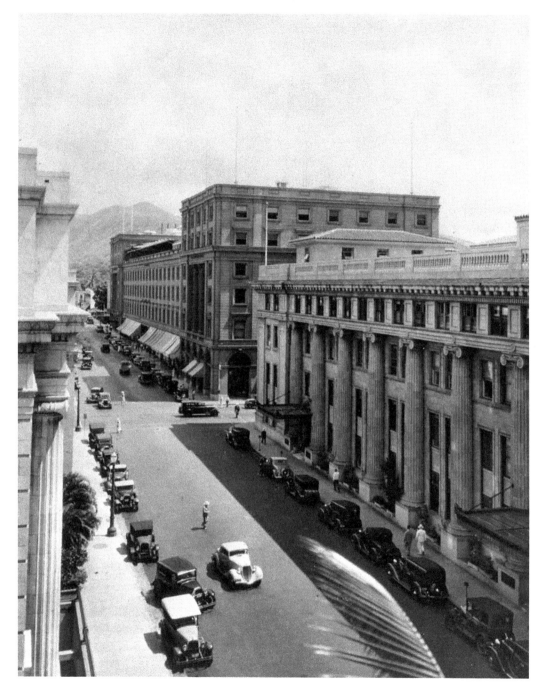

Despite the Depression and the large sums of money kept in the banks here on Bishop Street, Hawaii saw no bank robberies until February 3, 1934—and that took place at a Bank of Hawaii branch on Maui. The robbers were quickly caught and were sentenced to 20 years in prison. Most of the money they stole, slightly more than $975, was recovered.

The pilot Sir Charles Kingsford Smith, at right, and co-pilot Charles Ulm, at left, landed in Honolulu in 1934 on their way to Australia. In 1928 the two had made the historic first transpacific flight from the United States to Australia, a three-part journey during which they stopped in Hawaii.

Seen here in 1935, the Kress Building stood on Fort Street. Samuel H. Kress, founder of the Kress five-and-ten-cent store chain, donated a portion of his art collection to the Honolulu Academy of Arts. The museum, which opened in 1927, was founded by Anna Rice Cooke, wife of the politician and businessman Charles M. Cooke.

Seen here in 1935, the Arnott and Hough auto repair shop specialized in fixing Studebakers.

A variety of sturdy cars line Bishop Street in 1935. Honolulu developed a large automobile population rapidly, in part because to an island consciousness the idea of mobility was powerfully liberating. One benefit of having a car was the broader range of entertainment options it provided.

This 1935 scene of sail-rigged outrigger canoes along Waikiki is unusual. The Hawaiian outrigger canoe is designed to make quick turns and navigate along the coast, by evidence of its round hull and lack of a keel. The steering paddle serves as rudder and keel while the outrigger to leeward provides a stable course. The steersman must keep a watchful eye on the position of the outrigger and sail relative to the ocean swell. This is not an easy task, and because the canoes are small they are very unforgiving.

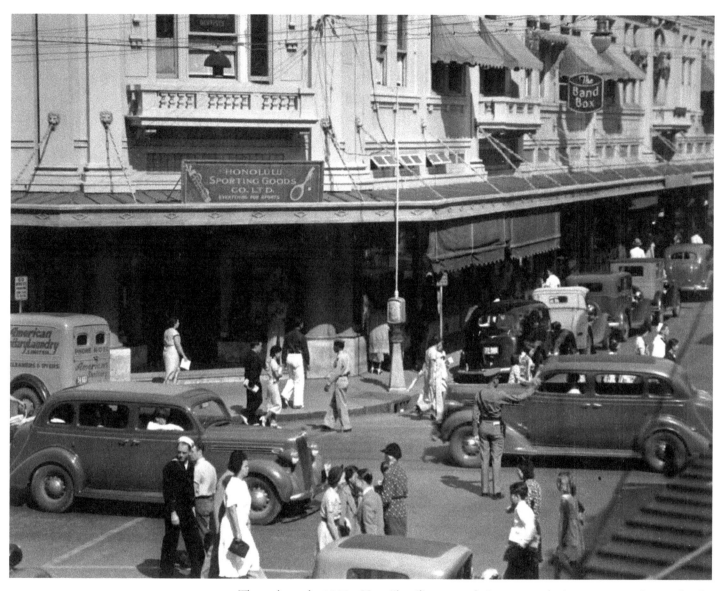

Throughout the 1930s, Hawaii's military population was on the increase, as can be seen by the number of servicemen walking past Honolulu Sporting Goods here in 1936. Their growing presence provided local residents with opportunity for a wider exposure to American culture. The military represented chivalry and honor, making it an admired profession for many Hawaiians.

The superstar actor and singer Bing Crosby visited Hawaii prior to starring in the 1937 film Waikiki Wedding, which was mostly filmed in California but featured Crosby singing "Sweet Leilani," a song he first heard played at the Royal Hawaiian Hotel in Honolulu. Written by Royal Hawaiian bandleader Harry Owens upon the birth of his daughter, "Sweet Leilani" won the Oscar for best original song. Crosby recorded the hit tune accompanied by Lani McIntire & His Hawaiians.

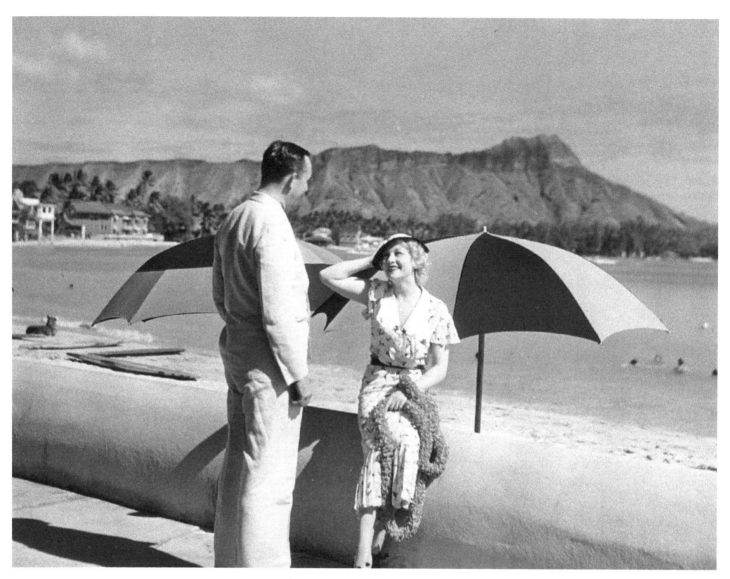

Fascination with Waikiki as an ultimate tourist destination affected the movie stars of the time. Here Betty Compson, a Hollywood star who had done some silent-film work in Hawaii in the 1920s, poses at the beach. Honolulu would become a second home to many movie stars and celebrities. In addition, the amount of filmmaking done in the islands through the years would help establish a small film industry, providing employment for local actors and writers.

Like banks did on Bishop Street, retailers lined Fort Street in 1938. People in Hawaii fared better than most during the Depression, mainly because demand for sugar was constant and labor was needed. Even so, Royal Credit Jewelers apparently determined that the only way to sell jewelry in Honolulu was on credit.

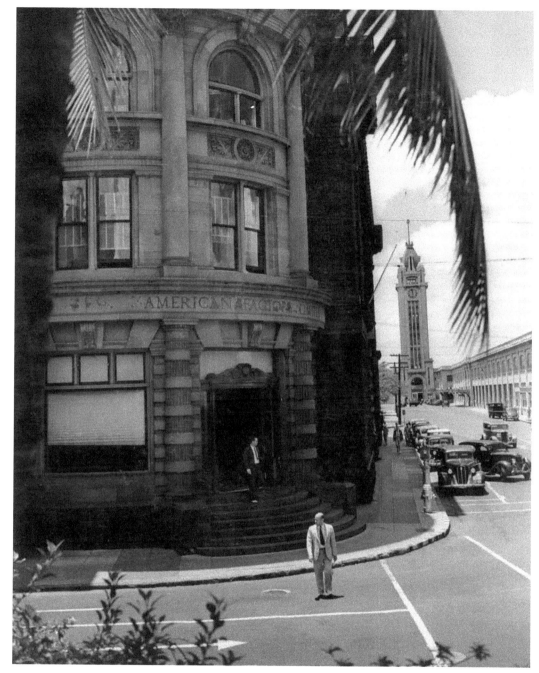

Seen here in 1939, the American Factors Building housed the Big Five company later known as Amfac. Among its many enterprises, American Factors was longtime parent company of the Liberty House retail chain.

Before dawn on December 7, 1941, when the Japanese attack began, eight of the nine battleships in the United States Navy fleet were anchored at Pearl Harbor. USS California, USS Maryland, USS Oklahoma, USS Tennessee, USS West Virginia, USS Nevada, and USS Arizona were positioned along Battleship Row. USS Pennsylvania was in dry dock.

Pearl Harbor and After

(1941–1950)

In dry dock astern of the badly hit destroyer USS Downes and the capsized destroyer USS Cassin, the Pennsylvania, flagship of the fleet, survived the attack with minimal damage and would be back in service within months.

The sneak attack of December 7, 1941, and the continued attacks on Hawaii as late as March of 1942 preyed heavily on the minds of those living in Honolulu. Fearful that the Japanese might invade Hawaii, many residents made plans for evacuation on ships leaving for the West Coast.

In a contrasting view from 1943, the Honolulu streets are virtually deserted.

On May 21, 1944, a second disaster at Pearl Harbor during World War II occurred at the West Loch Naval Magazine. A munitions explosion on one of 29 LST landing ships that had anchored at West Loch triggered a chain of fires on the nearby ships, ultimately killing 163 men and wounding 396. The LSTs were headed for the invasion of Saipan; in order to maintain the secrecy of their mission, the disaster at West Loch was kept quiet.

Here in 1944, with sidewalks full in the downtown shopping district, Honolulu could be mistaken for any peacetime city on a warm Saturday afternoon. In fact, Hawaii remained under martial law until October that year, as it had been since hours after the attack on Pearl Harbor.

In this 1947 aerial view, one can see clearly the enormity of Nuʻuanu Valley and picture how the water would flow into what became known as Honolulu Harbor. The carved valley walls act like flumes, sending captured rainwater into the harbor.

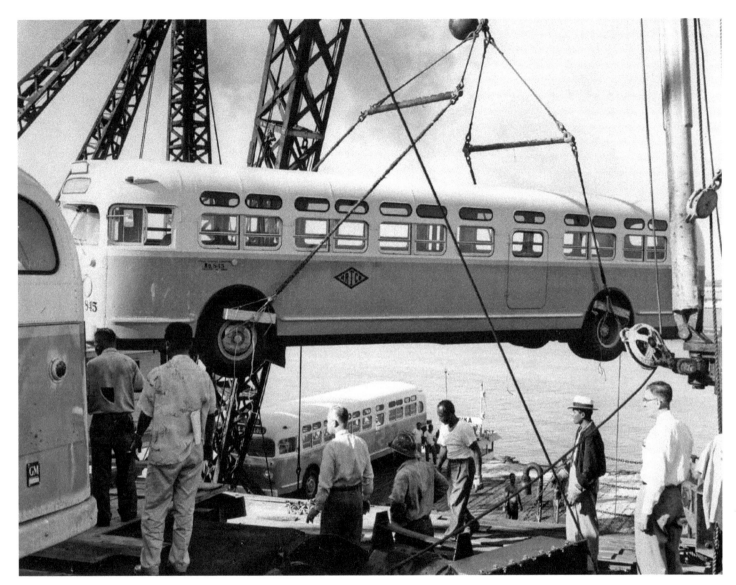

Like transit companies everywhere, Honolulu Rapid Transit found its trolley line aging and outmoded by the 1930s, and so began to offer bus service. But the company had agile competition in the form of small jitneys, so in 1940 the territorial public utilities commission granted Honolulu Rapid Transit a monopoly as a common carrier, forcing the popular jitney services to cease operation. Here, some years later, moving a fleet of Honolulu Rapid Transit buses is all in a day's work for these waterfront freight-handlers.

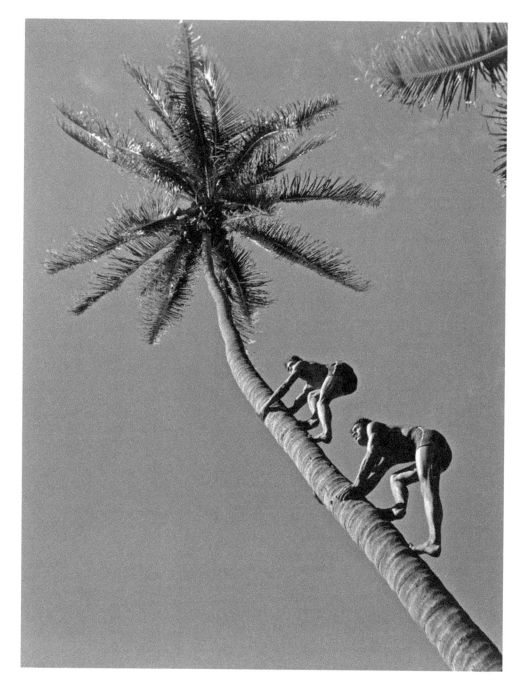

Popular with the Hawaiian community, the coconut served many purposes, including adaptation for use as a fishing buoy or portable water container. Dried, its shell could hold fishing hooks or be cut in half to serve as a cup. The outer husk of the coconut could be burned, and the ash was often used as a dye. Nevertheless, though a small industry existed, coconuts were never cultivated in Hawaii on a scale to compete with sugarcane and pineapples.

Notes on the Photographs

These notes, listed by page number, attempt to include all aspects known of the photographs. Each of the photographs is identified by the page number, a title or description, photographer and collection, archive, and call or box number when applicable. Although every attempt was made to collect all data, in some cases complete data may have been unavailable due to the age and condition of some of the photographs and records

Printed in the USA
CPSIA information can be obtained
at www.ICGtesting.com
JSHW072024140824
68134JS00042B/3775